MY CONFIRMATION JOURNAL

My CONFIRMATION JOURNAL

Bill & Patty Coleman

TWENTY-THIRD PUBLICATIONS

Mystic, Connecticut

Revised edition 1991

Twenty-Third Publications
P.O. Box 180
185 Willow Street
Mystic, CT 06355
(203) 536-2611

ISBN 0-89622-483-X

Dedication

To Angel and all who are bringing life
to their confirmation dreams
by working with the poor in foreign lands.

Contents

MY CONFIRMATION JOURNAL

Introduction

Congratulations! You are going to be confirmed. Confirmation is a milestone in your young Christian life. Some say that this sacrament is a sign of your maturity and a sign that the adult community of faith now takes you quite seriously.

Your teenage years are a wonderful time, a time of growth and discovery. You enter them a child and will emerge from them a young adult. You grow physically until you wonder whether you will ever have clothes that fit. You grow emotionally in self-control, in self-confidence, and in the ability to form friendships with many different kinds of people. You grow spiritually in your ability to love God and your neighbors.

All this growth is not without its special pain. There are days when you feel lonely and rejected, days when you are confused and unsure about your relationships with others, days when you even wonder about your own soul's life and vitality. Do not lose heart. God is with you. You are God's special friend, loved and cared for more than you can imagine.

In the sacrament of confirmation, God will confirm this great love for you, saying once more, "You are my own child, made in my own image, the brother or sister of my son, Jesus. I am well pleased with what I have created and I love you tenderly."

As you prepare to hear God's words spoken through the sacrament, we hope this journal will be of help to you. It is not a classroom book, not something you will do to please

other people, but your own book. Here you can write down
your inner thoughts and your deepest feelings. Here you
can discover the whisperings of God within your heart.
Here you can plan for the future, ponder the meaning of the
past, and make the present a vivid memory for the days
ahead.

There are eight chapters in this book. Each is meant to be
read and pondered for several days. You can read from
your journal before you go to bed at night and sketch in it
some of your best thoughts. Stay with a single chapter as
long as it is helping you grow closer to God.

In each chapter are a few words about growth, some
questions to help you think about life, prayers to say, Bible
readings to ponder, the story of an interesting saint, some
ideas to discuss with others, and a final word about the future. We hope each of these will help you in your prayer
and inner search.

We have one request to make of you as you prepare for
confirmation. It is that you remember Bill and Patty who
wrote this book for you.

1

Who Am I?

Do you ever feel like a mirror? Many teenagers say they do. A mirror sits waiting for people to come by and reflect their images in it. It has no image of its own. When no one is present it has no life of its own.

We feel like a mirror when our parents reflect their own dreams for us. They praise us when we are successful in school or when we win a game. They are disappointed with us when we fail in school or lose an important game. Then they go away and we are left alone to await the next person who will reflect his or her image on us.

Perhaps the next person is a teacher who tells us we are good when we behave in class or complete an assignment. Later the same teacher may tell us we are less than good when we slip and misbehave or forget an important assignment. Soon the teacher, too, is gone and we are once more alone with only the memory of her reflections.

Next, our friends come by. They tell us we are great because we have new clothes or the latest CDs. Another time they tell us that we are out of it because our clothes are ugly, our hair styled the wrong way, or our music out of date. They, like the others, go away and leave us with nothing to reflect.

Who are we? Are we the good person our parents, teachers and friends sometimes see? Or are we the failures these same people also claim to see within us? Even if there were no parents, teachers, and friends, would we not still be something? Isn't there something more to us than what other people tell us about ourselves?

That's the great question. Are we more than mirrors, more than a reflection of other people's ideas of us? Are we unique and special even when no one seems to notice us?

Finding the answer to that important question is what growing up is all about. Psychologists say that the great task of adolescence is discovering our own identity and enjoying it. They tell us that only when we can be more than a mirror of what other people think about us will we be fully grown.

Our task during our adolescent years, then, is to become more than a mirror. We must become like a picture that shows others what it is, not what they want it to become. We must discover our real personality and project it outward because inside we are at peace with who and what we are.

There are clues to answering the "Who are we?" question in the Bible, in the long traditions of our church, and in the insights of modern science. We can read a great deal about what it means to be human, but we must then apply all this to ourselves and discover whether or not this is true for us.

No other person can tell us who we are, not our parents, our teachers, or our friends. We must discover that by ourselves. Good luck in your search for an answer. Nothing in life is more important and nothing more exciting than the search for your own inner self.

Thinking About Yourself

1. Can you think of three times during the past week you have been really happy? Jot them down.

    1. _____
    2. _____
    3. _____

2. Why did each of these times make you feel happy? Jot down your reasons.

    1. _____
    2. _____
    3. _____

3. Can you think of seven things that would make you happy right now? Jot them down.

    1. _____
    2. _____
    3. _____
    4. _____
    5. _____
    6. _____
    7. _____

4. Were any of your seven things about people?
    Yes ____ No ____

5. Were any about achieving success?
    Yes ____ No ____

6. Were any about your parents?

     Yes ⎯⎯ No ⎯⎯

7. Were any about owning things?

     Yes ⎯⎯ No ⎯⎯

Your answers to these questions should tell you something about what you want in life. The things that make us happy are the things we most desire.

Prayers

To God About Myself

Dear God,

You know more about me than I know about myself.

You can see beneath the person I pretend to be.

You can see the kernel of personality

     which is the real me.

And you love what you see.

You love me even when I am not sure I love myself.

Help me to see myself as you see me, Lord.

And help me to like myself so that one day I may really like
     others, too.

Thank you, God, for all your help.

Amen.

To God When I Am Lonely

Dear God,

I am sometimes like a mirror.

I reflect what others say and do.

I am happy when all around me smile.

I am sad when frowning faces swirl around me.

I am filled with courage if others are brave.

And I am a little weak when cowardice holds me in chains.

Most of all, I find it hard to be alone where there is no one to reflect in this mirror which is me.

Help me find who and what I am so that I need be a mirror no more.

Help me become a striking picture of the real me,

a picture I will admire and be proud to be,

a picture made in your own image as the Bible says,

a picture I can love and show you proudly.

Help me, God. Amen.

Bible Readings

Here are two short readings from the Bible to help you think more about who and what you are.

Ancient people also wondered who they were. In the first chapter of Genesis (1:26–27), God gave them this important clue:

God said, "Let us make people in our own image, in the likeness of ourselves, and let them be masters of the fish of the sea, the birds of heaven, the cattle, all the wild beasts and all the reptiles that crawl upon the earth."

God created humankind in God's own image, in that image God created them, male and female God created them.

What does this passage tell you about being human?

_____

_____

_____

Do you ever think of yourself as made in the image of God?

_____

_____

_____

Can anything made in the image of God be useless? Why?

_____

_____

_____

Does it make you feel good to be made this way? Why?

_____

_____

_____

Saint Paul understood how we sometimes feel. He contrasted our understanding now with what it will be when we are with God. These are Paul's words (1 Corinthians 13:12):

> Now we are seeing a dim reflection in a mirror; but then we shall be seeing face to face. The knowledge that I have now is imperfect; but then I shall know as fully as I am known.

How is your knowledge dim and like an imperfect mirror?

_____

_____

_____

What things do you know about yourself?

_____

_____

_____

Do you like what you know about yourself? Why?

_____

_____

_____

These are good Bible readings to think about during the day. Return to them often, and ask yourself what they say about who and what you are.

A Saint for Now

Maria Goretti
(1890–1902)

If ever a girl had reason to believe she did not count for much, that girl was Maria Goretti. Maria's family was poor, poorer than most people today could even imagine. Her father had no education. He worked as a tenant farmer in Italy, moving from one farm to another. Before Maria was nine, she and her five brothers and sisters had moved onto three different farms. Each time she had to make new friends and adjust to even greater poverty. For the Goretti family, even food was in short supply. Their homes were poor shacks without heat, electricity, or even running water.

Because the Gorettis were so poor, none of the children could go to school. Maria could neither read nor write.

When Maria was ten years old, even greater tragedy struck her family. Her father died. Now the family had no income except what her mother could earn working in the fields. These were the days before welfare payments and social security benefits. Poor families had no security and very little food.

After her husband's death, Maria's mother took her husband's place in the fields. She went to work before dawn and returned home only after the sun had set. Maria, only ten at the time, became the housekeeper and mother to her brothers and sisters. She was alone all day long with the younger children.

In spite of her terrible poverty and her weighty obligations, Maria grew into a relaxed, happy, and self-confident girl. She was not frightened by those who lived around her, nor did she feel inferior to anyone. She knew who she was and insisted on being respected as the good person she knew she was. Even older people admired the calm composure on the face of the girl now grown to twelve.

Near the Gorettis lived another poor farming family with a son named Alessandro. Alessandro was seven years older than Maria, a brutal, brawling, often drunken man. All the composure and self-confidence that shone in Maria's face was absent in Alessandro's.

Alessandro often came by to visit Maria. Maria was cool and reserved with him. Alessandro would try to show off for her with great feats of strength. Maria ignored him. The more she ignored him, the more infatuated with her he became. Soon he tried to tempt her to have sex with him. Maria stoutly refused. She knew what was right and wrong and knew, too, how she felt about this strange young man.

One warm July day, Alessandro came back to Maria. This

time he was armed with a deadly knife. He pointed it at Maria and demanded that she have sex with him. Maria refused. Alessandro stabbed her not once but many times. Still Maria remained firm in her refusal. Finally, Alessandro fled in confusion and shame, leaving her dying on the kitchen floor.

The next day Maria died. Before her death, however, the twelve-year-old girl forgave her murderer and even prayed for him. Not long after her death, people in the area said she was a saint and began to pray to her. Their prayers were answered and miracle after miracle began to happen. While Maria's mother was still living, Maria was canonized a saint by the church.

Maria is a good saint to know about, not only because she knew right from wrong, but because she never forgot her own goodness and importance in the eyes of God. She knew that God loved and cared for her even though she lived in the midst of poverty, violence, and broken dreams.

Ideas to Discuss with Others

We can learn many important lessons from those who share our lives. To learn the lessons we must listen to their experiences and their wisdom. Parents, especially, are good sources for our growth in self-understanding. Here are a few questions you might like to ask others. When you hear their answers, ponder them during your quiet moments.

Questions for Your Parents
When you were my age, how did you feel about yourself? Did you ever feel embarrassed and unsure? How did you

cope with these feelings? Was there anything particular that helped you achieve self-confidence? How do you feel about yourself now? Are your feelings different from what they were when you were my age?

Questions for a Teacher

Why do you work with young people? Do you think you are helping us grow? Do you ever wonder what other people think of you? What do you do when others do not like you?

Questions for a Friend

How do you feel about being our age? Were you happier or sadder when you were ten? What makes you feel this way now? Do you think other young people feel as you do?

Questions for God

How do you feel about me? Am I maturing as you wish me to? Is there anything more I could be doing to please you?

A Final Word

Soon you will be confirmed. Confirmation means firming something up, strengthening it. One way of looking at the sacrament is that we "firm up" our belief in God and God's son, Jesus. Another way of thinking about this same sacrament is that God and the Christian community confirm and strengthen us. Like all sacraments, confirmation is a two-way affair.

We are to love God with our whole heart, our entire mind, and all our strength. Jesus taught us this. At confirmation, we say we will try to grow into this kind of love for God. Of course, we cannot predict the future and cannot be sure just what will happen to us. Yet, we can say that we will *try*. That is our part of the sacrament.

A more important part of the sacrament is God's promise to help us by strengthening us and firming up our ability to love. That love we receive at confirmation is God, for the Bible teaches us that God is love. Theologians tell us that in confirmation the Holy Spirit comes to dwell within us in a special way. Imagine that! God dwelling within us. What reason for confidence! What reason to be sure we are never alone!

As you prepare for confirmation, think often of the wonderful gift God will bring to you. The more you ponder how much this sacrament can give to you, the more you will receive from it. God is waiting to firm up your personality. All that is needed is for you to ask God's help.

2

Who Is This God?

Do you ever wonder about God? Do you ever ask these questions? What is God like? What does God think of me?

Jesus told us that God the Father is like the father in the story of the prodigal son. Other passages in the Bible tell us that God is even more understanding than most earthly fathers. In fact, God's love is so tender and so forgiving that we can call God our mother, too. Whether it is easier to think of God as our father or our mother is not that important. What is important is that we understand that God loves us even more than any earthly parent can.

Some say God is powerful, and they are right. Others think of God as kind and loving. They, too, are right. The Bible tells us that God created heaven and earth, everything. What could be more powerful than that? The same Bible also tells us that God sent Jesus to share our lives and be our brother. What could be more kind and loving?

In the Bible account and in the tradition of the church, we learn that God is mysterious: both powerful and kind, both merciful and just, one and yet somehow three. This boggles

---

our minds. You and I are each one human being with a name that sums up our own unique personality. God, however, is one divine being but with three names that tell us God has three unique personalities and still is one God.

The first of God's names is *Father*. This person in God is the one we think about when we talk of creation and sending the son. The second of God's names is *Son*. It is the son, we know, who came to be our brother. His human name was Jesus. God's third name is *Spirit*. It is the Holy Spirit we think about when we talk of confirmation, the church, and the work of making people holy in their daily lives. Of course, this is only our human way of thinking. Whatever God does in our world involves all three persons; otherwise God would not be perfectly One. Yet for our human minds, thinking of the three persons of God in this way is helpful.

God the Father is, Jesus told us, like the father of the prodigal son who loves his children intensely and is willing to forgive them any sin if they are sorry. Similarly God cares for us in every detail of our lives. Jesus says that our Father even numbers the hairs on our heads. Kindness and concern, then, are words that help us understand the Father.

Jesus is *God the Son* become a human being. Once we know the stories of Jesus, we can understand the Son of God. He is our own brother, a friend, one who loves us so much he was willing to die for us.

The *Holy Spirit* or, as we sometimes say, the *Spirit of God* is the person who first energized the church at Pentecost, the person who today dwells within us, the person who makes all members of the church holy. The spirit is sometimes called the spirit of love because God is love.

Each time we make the sign of the cross, say the Nicene Creed at Mass, or any one of many prayers, we profess our belief in the three persons of God who are one. In our own private prayer, we find that sometimes we can talk to the Father most easily. At other times, we find our prayer to Jesus or the Holy Spirit the best approach. It does not really matter to which person we pray. What is important is that we pray and realize how close God, in all three persons, is to us.

Being a Christian, then, opens up to us three persons to whom we can talk. Prayer is easier for us because of this threeness in God. Because it is easier, God expects that we will take advantage of this opportunity and pray often to the Father, the Son, and the Holy Spirit.

Thinking About God

1. Become very quiet and in the space below draw the word GOD slowly. Play with the letters. Draw around them. Take your time and savor your feelings.

2. How did you feel when you wrote God's name? Happy or sad? _____

Why do you think you felt that way? _____

_____

_____

Frightened or secure? _____

Why do you think you felt that way? _____

_____

_____

Do you love God?_____

Why do you think you love or don't love God? _____

_____

_____

3. Think for a few minutes about Jesus. How do you feel when you think of him?_____

_____

_____

Why do you think you feel this way? _____

_____

_____

4. Think for several minutes about the Holy Spirit. How do you feel when you think of this third person of God?

_____

_____

_____

Why do you think you feel this way?_____

_____

_____

Prayers

To God About God

God, I know that you are three.

I know you are the *Father* who created all.

I know you are the *Son* who became my human brother.

I know you are the *Holy Spirit* who makes the world holy.

I know all this but I do not understand.

I think of you as my loving Father, as my brother, and as
my daily companion through life.

This is enough for me.

I am content to be with you, though I don't understand.

Be with me all the days of my life and for all eternity. Amen.

To God, My Loving Parent

God, you are my first parent,
   the one who gave me life,
   the one who cares for me each day,
   the one who reaches out to me with love.
I rejoice to have you as my parent.
Because of you, I am at peace.
I do not fear life and its uncertainties.
You are with me through them all.
Help me to live in such a way that others will recognize in me the image of my parent and give you glory because of me. Amen.

Bible Readings

Here are two short readings from the Bible to help you think more about God.

On the night before Jesus died, he comforted his grieving and frightened apostles when he said (John 14:1, 3):

Do not let your hearts be troubled. Trust in God still, and trust in me....I am going now to prepare a place for you, and after I have gone and prepared you a place, I shall return to take you with me; so that where I am you may be too.

What does this reading say to you about God? _____

_____

_____

_____

Do you think God cares for you and has a special place for you? _____

_____

_____

Do you feel happy and secure when you think about God? Why? Why not? _____

_____

_____

_____

In another passage, we can read about all the persons of God and their concern for us. Jesus speaks (John 14:23, 25, 26):

Those who love me will keep my word,
and my Father will love them,
and we shall come to them
and make our home with those persons.
I have said these things to you
while still with you;
but the Advocate, the Holy Spirit,
whom the Father will send in my name,
will teach you everything
and remind you of all I have said to you.

How do you show you love Jesus? _____

_____

_____

How does God show love for you? _____

_____

_____

Do you ever think of God living within you? _____
_____
_____

Do you ever feel that the Holy Spirit reminds you of Jesus
during the day? _____
_____
_____

Write your own prayer in the space below. In it, tell God
how you really feel. _____
_____
_____
_____
_____
_____
_____
_____

A Saint for Now

Francis de Sales
(1567–1622)

Many people believe they are too busy to think about God.
Not so young Francis. Wherever he went and whatever he
did, Francis found ways to think about God.

Francis was born into a wealthy and important family in
France over 400 years ago. He was a bright, cheerful boy, always on the move, always interested in learning something
new. Both his father and his mother had great dreams for
young Francis. When he was ten years old, he received his
first communion and his confirmation on the same day. It

was an important day for Francis who even as a child was keenly aware of God in his life.

Later Francis's parents sent him off to college, to the great University of Paris. There he studied a little bit of everything, the arts, history, science, theology, and anything else his teachers seemed to enjoy teaching. He had an almost boundless appetite for information.

After college, he returned home to visit with his family. His father wanted young Francis to become a government official and exercise influence on national and world affairs. Francis had a different idea; he wanted to become a priest. His father refused to allow Francis to become a priest. After hours of discussion, Francis agreed to attend a different university to study law. This, his father thought, would fit him for a career in government.

While Francis was studying law, he began to think more seriously about God. He drew up a rule of life for himself. Each day he spent some time in prayer, some time in reading the Bible, some time in helping others. He did all this and his school work, too. His fellow students loved the gentle Francis. He never seemed too pious for a good joke or a long conversation. He seemed to enjoy life even more than they did.

After earning his law degree, Francis went to his father once more. They discussed his future and this time his father allowed young Francis to become a priest. Francis was such a gifted priest that soon he was named bishop. Before long, people from all over Europe were coming to him for advice and inspiration. Francis never refused to help any person who came to him or wrote him a letter.

What was so remarkable about Francis was not his zeal and endless activities but his determination to remember

God in everything he did. An hour rarely went by that Francis did not think quietly about God's goodness and love for him. He asked himself over and over again what he could do to be more like Jesus. As he grew older, people said Francis was a saintly man not simply because of his good deeds but because he was always composed, always smiling, and gently joyful.

In his lifetime Francis wrote 26 volumes of essays and letters. He was a very active bishop. He helped the poor, the powerless, and those in need of counseling. He was known all over Europe as one of the wisest and best men of his time. Yet, all this happened because Francis first talked regularly with God and in all his activity never forgot that loving God was the most important task in his life.

Today we call this man Saint Francis de Sales, the patron saint of those who write about God.

Ideas to Discuss with Others

We can learn many important lessons from those who share our lives. To learn the lessons we must listen to their experiences and their wisdom. Parents, especially, are good sources for our growth in understanding God. Here are a few questions you might like to ask others. When you hear their answers, ponder them during your quiet moments.

Questions for Your Parents
Do you think about God during the day? Have you learned to talk to God in your own words? What sort of things do you say? Whom do you pray for? What kind of things do you ask God to give you? Do you ever pray for me? How can I learn to pray during the day?

Questions for a Teacher

What do you think about God? Does God seem kind and loving to you? Are you ever afraid of God? Do you think God will punish us for our mistakes? Why? Do you think God will forgive us easily?

Questions for a Friend

What do you think God is like? Do you think God would be happy in our group? Do you ever pray? How do you go about it?

Questions for God

Why do you love me so very much? How can I learn to love you at least a little more?

A Final Word

You are God's own child, God's special friend. So deeply and with such concern does God love you that you can say "My Father...my mother...my very own friend." All this makes you a very special person.

When you understand how much God loves you, your life changes. You feel confident and good inside. You are able to reach out to other people and help them. You are able to be at rest within yourself. You have that peace which Jesus says surpasses all understanding.

In a few weeks God will confirm a great love for you. As the bishop reads the words of the confirmation ritual and anoints your forehead with holy chrism, God will touch your heart in a special way. God will bring you courage and confidence, joy and peace. After confirmation, you will have yet another reminder of the overwhelming love God has for you.

Your part in preparing for confirmation is primarily one of prayer. Prayer begins when we realize God is with us. We cannot have a conversation with God until we know God is present. As long as we allow our daily cares and worries to fill our minds, we do not have room for God. God comes to us when we are quiet and still, ready for a conversation.

In these weeks before confirmation, try to spend some little time being quiet. Do this each day. It may be before you fall asleep or first thing in the morning, or walking home from school, or on the school bus. Just find one time and, each day, spend it quietly with God. You will never regret these moments and will look back upon them as some of the most wonderful in your life.

3

Miracles Without Magic

Have you ever been to a magic show? If so, you have seen what seemed like miracles. Empty hats produced rabbits. Someone seemed to be sawed in half and put back together again. Someone else disappeared only to reappear where you least expected it. Magicians seem very powerful and terribly clever.

Some people think of God as a kind of magician, expecting tricks performed for them when they need them. They pray for good weather because they have a ball game scheduled and expect God to manipulate the clouds to keep the rain away. Perhaps they are failing in school because they have not done their work and then ask God to choose for their examination only the questions they can answer. This is a silly way to think about God. God is not a magician we can call in to help us and then forget about when we have no further need.

No, God does not ordinarily do anything like magic, but rather builds on the nature already created. God strengthens people so they can bear pain, gives courage to those who are timid so they can accomplish the tasks in their lives, helps leaders realize their best potential. God doesn't perform magic, but rather builds up our personalities in a remarkable way.

When you prepare for the sacrament of confirmation, this is a good idea to keep in mind. In this sacrament, God will help you change and become a better person, but will not perform some magic over you. Working with your personality, not against it, God will help and enable you but never take away your own responsibility for your life.

God's power is like the power of a friend who loves us. When we are loved by a friend, we are enabled to become our very best selves. All the natural powers within us are freed to work in the formation of our personality. This is the sort of thing which can happen to us in confirmation if we will allow it.

Confirmation is a reminder of the great love God has for us, but it is even more than that. In confirmation God will come to live within us in a special way, loving us even more than we can love ourselves.

If we will open our hearts to this love of God for us, then we will change. Some writers call these changes the fruits and gifts of the Holy Spirit. They include things like peace, joy, patience, love, and other virtues. God's loving us builds up all that is already potentially good in our personalities which God has already created and graced at baptism.

Our part in preparing for confirmation is to be sure we allow God to love us and to be sure we are aware of the awesome power God's sacrament brings into our lives. We can get ready for confirmation by learning more about this God who loves us so and by imitating God's concern for the poor and the downtrodden. When we reach out to help others, we become more and more like God. We can also become more aware of God by praying and working in this journal and by talking to God in the quiet moments of our day.

Confirmation is a wonderful time in our lives, a time when we come very close to God. There is nothing magical about our Father in heaven and the Holy Spirit. God's power is much stronger than magic. It is the power to warm our hearts when they are chilled, the power to put courage into us when we are weak, the power to help us grow into men and women whose lives are like the life of Jesus.

Thinking About Confirmation

1. List below five things about your personality that are very good:

a. _____

b. _____

c. _____

d. _____

e. _____

2. In the space below, write a prayer thanking God for the good things in your personality.

Dear God, I thank you _____

_____

_____

_____

_____

_____

_____

_____

3. Write the name of the adult person you most admire.

_____

_____

4. What do you admire about this person?_____

_____

_____

_____

5. In what ways are you already like him or her? _____

_____

_____

_____

6. Write a prayer asking God to help you grow to be more like your model.

Dear God, _____

_____

_____

_____

_____

_____

_____

Prayers

A Pentecostal Prayer

Here I am, God.
There are sights and sounds
    of fire and wind.
There are the timid suddenly turned brave.
Pentecost and all its power are here

for me to savor and enjoy today.
May my heart be open to the joy of other hearts.
May I, like them, share the news of Jesus
    with anyone who will listen,
    with anyone who can believe.
Amen, Amen.

To God About Confirmation

God, our Father,
    pour out the gifts of your Holy Spirit on us.
As you sent your spirit on that first Pentecost
    to begin the teaching of the gospel,
    so now let the Spirit continue that work in each of us.
Help us grow into fully mature persons
    who love the gospel and Jesus, the Gospel maker.
We ask you this in his name. Amen.

A Prayer for Help

Direct, we beseech you, O God,
    every thought, word, and deed of ours,
    so that when each has begun in you
    it may, through the assistance of your Spirit,
    be ended happily.
We ask this in the name of Jesus, the Lord. Amen.

Bible Readings

Here are two short readings from the Bible to help you
think more about confirmation.

On Pentecost Sunday (50 days after Jesus had risen from
the dead) the Holy Spirit came upon Jesus' friends in a very

special way. This day was to these early followers of Jesus what our confirmation can be for us (Acts of the Apostles 2:1–4).

> When Pentecost day came round, they all met in one room, when suddenly they heard what sounded like a powerful wind from heaven, the noise of which filled the entire house in which they were sitting; and something appeared to them which seemed like tongues of fire; these separated and came to rest on the head of each of them. They were all filled with the Holy Spirit.

How do you think the friends of Jesus felt when they heard this strange noise and saw the tongues of fire? _____

_____

What does it mean to you to be filled with the Holy Spirit?

_____

_____

What do you hope the Holy Spirit will do in your life when you are confirmed? _____

_____

_____

In another passage from the Acts of the Apostles (8:4,5,14–17) we read of what may have been the first sacramental confirmation.

> Those who had escaped [the persecution of the church in Jerusalem] went from place to place preaching the

Good News. One of them was Philip who went to a Samaritan town and proclaimed the Christ to them. The people united in welcoming the message Philip preached....

When the apostles in Jerusalem heard that Samaria had accepted the word of God, they sent Peter and John to Samaria, and they went down there and prayed for the Samaritans to receive the Holy Spirit, for as yet he had not come down on any of them: they had only been baptized in the name of the Lord Jesus. Then Peter and John laid hands on the Samaritans, and they received the Holy Spirit.

What did the Samaritan people have to do first in order to be ready for confirmation? _____

_____

_____

What do you need to do to prepare yourself for confirmation?

_____

_____

_____

_____

A Saint for Now

Oscar Romero
(1917–1980)

El Salvador is a tiny country on the Pacific coast south of Mexico and Guatemala. Once its fertile land supported many different tribes of native Americans. When the Spanish conquered Mexico and Guatemala in the sixteenth century, they swallowed up the people in this area as well and established a capital, San Salvador, which meant Holy Savior. Time and time again over the centuries, Spanish settlers and, later, Salvadoran rulers lashed out against the camposinos, or peasants, whom they considered their slaves.

One year, 1932, word went out from the dictator that all who protested unjust treatment would be killed. No one is sure how many were murdered that year but we are sure that very many died, many in one massacre.

Oscar Romero was a teenager when that massacre occurred. He heard people talk of it, saw churches that were destroyed during battles, and absorbed the official history of the conflict in school and at home. Like most of his fellow citizens, Oscar bore the scars of 1932.

When he became a priest and later a bishop, he tried to shy away from the politics of his nation. The slaughter of 1932, he feared, might occur again, and many innocent people would die needlessly.

When Oscar Romero was appointed the archbishop of San Salvador in 1977, most people believed that he would be a quiet, retiring spiritual leader and nothing more. In the first years of his service in San Salvador, he began renovating the cathedral and looking after traditional church programs. He was a quiet, sincere man who minded his own affairs and said little about the war which was already engulfing El Salvador.

Then God touched his heart and called on him to change. When soldiers of the Salvadoran army arrested one of the priests of his diocese and tortured him, Oscar Romero knew he must speak out. From that moment on, his life was never the same.

Archbishop Romero turned his seminary into a place of refuge for poor people fleeing the war. He began speaking out against the brutal atrocities of the government. His sermons were broadcast to every corner of the country because they contained the only news most people were allowed to hear about the war. He even wrote to the United States president and asked him to stop sending arms to the government of the tiny, war-torn nation.

The powerful in El Salvador, the rich and the army, were outraged that their archbishop should side with the poor against them. Some of them plotted to kill him. When he asked the soldiers of El Salvador to refuse to kill their own people, the powerful had had enough. The next day, they sent an assassin to shoot the archbishop while he was saying Mass in a local hospital. Oscar Romero died a martyr for justice and for his beloved people.

Many Salvadorans consider him their special saint. Everyone who is to be confirmed can see in him the kind of courage and love which the sacrament of confirmation brings into our lives.

Ideas to Discuss with Others

We can learn many important lessons from those who share our lives. To learn the lessons we must listen to their experiences and their wisdom. Parents especially are good sources for our growth in understanding about life. Here are a few questions you might like to ask others. When you hear their answers, ponder them during your quiet moments.

Questions for Your Parents
Do you remember your own confirmation? How old were

you when you were confirmed? How did you feel before
confirmation? Were you excited? How did you feel after
you were confirmed? Can you remember the bishop who
confirmed you? Are you excited about my being confirmed? Why?

Questions for a Teacher

Do you enjoy helping boys and girls get ready for confirmation? Why? What does confirmation mean to you? Can you
remember your own confirmation? What do you remember
most about your confirmation?

Questions for a Friend

What do you think about when you think about confirmation? What saint's name will you take for confirmation?
Why?

Questions for God

How will you help me in the sacrament of confirmation?
How can I prepare to take advantage of the help you want
to offer me?

A Final Word

Confirmation is a special time in your life. It is a time of
hope and promise. You have great powers within you, powers that have not yet begun to assert themselves. You have
the power to think and make sense of life. You have the
power to love unselfishly. You have the power to feel pain,
sorrow, joy, and enthusiasm.

All these powers that God has already given you will be
heightened by the coming of the Holy Spirit in confirma-

tion. Your power to think will grow deeper. Because of your friendship with the Spirit of God, you will come to understand more and more about God and God's extraordinary love for you. You will also grow in your ability to love other people, parents, friends, the poor, and those most in need of tender compassion.

The Spirit of God will also help you to become more sensitive. You will feel pain more easily because you love more deeply. When you see people hungry, hurt, or broken by life, you will experience some of their pain. You will also know sorrow when you see how your own actions sometimes influence the lives of other people. Because you will become ever more sensitive, you will know some pain and some sorrow.

Yet that pain and sorrow will be small compared with the great joy and enthusiasm which will flood into your life if you will allow it. God's love will remake your whole way of looking at life. Once you understand how real and how true a friend God is to you, your joy will know no bounds. Once you understand how close God can be, you will be filled with an enthusiasm for living you did not think possible before.

Yes, confirmation is a special time in your young life. Treasure it.

4

Courage to Speak Out

Have you ever wanted to ask a question in class and had the words get caught in your throat? You wanted to ask but somehow you felt too embarrassed to say the words. This happens to many young people. They are so afraid others will laugh at them or think them silly they clam up and say nothing.

Saint Luke's gospel tells the story of Jesus as a young adolescent. When Jesus was twelve years old he made his initial trip to the temple in Jerusalem. For the first time he was allowed to enter into the part of the temple reserved for the men of Israel. To be twelve and in the temple was a momentous thing for a young Jewish boy.

Like the other boys his age, Jesus sat with the learned rabbis and listened to them talk about the law. The boys were expected to ask questions of the rabbis and then to listen to their answers. All the adults sat nearby and listened to them dialogue with the learned men. Few boys asked many questions for, like boys of every age, they were afraid of appearing silly or stupid.

Jesus was different. He asked many questions. In fact, the more questions he asked the more questions popped into his mind. Hour after hour he asked and listened. Every answer created new problems and new questions. The older people who watched his young mind at work marveled at his wisdom.

What happened to Jesus is often true of any young person. Once we overcome our shyness and find the courage to speak out, we are as wise as anyone else. Our big problem is finding the courage to forget what others will think of us if we make a mistake.

One of the gifts the Holy Spirit brings to us in the sacrament of confirmation is the gift of courage. The Holy Spirit helps us understand how loved we are and so how little it matters if anyone laughs at us or thinks we are stupid. This is the courage that enabled young people of other ages to become martyrs and even now gives many people, where Christians are persecuted and elsewhere, the ability to take great risks for Jesus.

The problems we face in speaking out usually are not nearly so dramatic as those of the martyrs or those of youth in totalitarian countries today. Most of our problems come because we fear being rejected by people our own age. In school we often "freeze up" when it is time to discuss new ideas. In conversation with others, we often refrain from saying what we really feel. When our group is about to do something we do not approve of, we often say nothing and just go along because we do not want to be thought of as different or too "good."

The Holy Spirit will help us with these problems when we receive confirmation. The Holy Spirit will not perform magic for us, but will help us outgrow these childish fears. The Spirit will help us understand that we need not be embarrassed all the time, and that we have the right to speak what we believe.

We cooperate with the Spirit of God by praying for courage and by trying to practice it in little ways. We can begin by refusing to go along with a group when it is planning something wrong. We can get ready for later life by learning to ask questions in class even if we do appear a little silly. We can practice telling the truth with our friends even if they do not always appreciate it. With the help of the Holy Spirit and our own practice, courage to speak out will soon be ours.

Thinking About Fears

1. Imagine yourself with a group of your friends who are talking about trying drugs? Would you have the courage to say it is a foolish thing to do? Why do you think you would or would not? _____

_____

_____

_____

_____

2. How do you feel when:
a. Someone says you are too fat, or too thin?_____

_____

b. Someone accuses you of being too "good"? _____

_____

c. Someone laughs at your favorite idea?_____

_____

d. A teacher makes fun of you in class?_____

_____

3. Do you ever fail to say what you think because you are afraid of what others will say about you? When? _____

_____

_____

_____

4. Think about your answers to the questions above and write a prayer to the Holy Spirit for *courage to speak out.*

Spirit of God, who gave the apostles the courage to speak out before the whole world, _____

_____

_____

_____

_____

_____

_____

Prayers

To the Holy Spirit for Courage

God the Holy Spirit,
Hear my prayer for courage.
I am not always the outspoken, courageous person
   I want to be.
I am often afraid of what others will say,
   of giggling laughter when I speak,
   of put-downs and silly looks.

All these fears of mine keep me from doing good and
   being more like Jesus.

Help me with your gift of courage to speak out.

Put fire into my heart and let me overcome my shyness
   and pain.

Make of me a witness to Jesus and the truth of life.

Heal my wounded heart. Amen.

Signs of Love

Lord, our kindly parent,

Help us become a symbol of your love.

Let all who see us be impressed by our sincerity

   By the temper of our gentleness

   And the true light of our concern.

Help us to be signs of love

   Love with and in you

   Love among us all.

Amen. Amen.

Bible Readings

Here are two short readings from the Bible to help you
think more about the courage to speak out the Holy Spirit
brings into our lives.

When Jesus was twelve years old, he had great personal
courage because the Spirit of his Father lived within him
(Luke 2:41–42, 46–47).

Every year his parents used to go to Jerusalem for the
feast of the Passover. When he was twelve years old
they went up for the feast as usual. When they were on

their way home after the feast, the boy Jesus stayed behind in Jerusalem without his parents knowing it....Three days later, they found him in the temple, sitting among the doctors, listening to them and asking them questions; and all those who heard him were astonished at his intelligence and his replies.

Does this sound like something you might do? Why? Why not? _____

_____

_____

Would you have the courage to ask questions of teachers and other educated people? Why? Why not?_____

_____

_____

Do you have the courage to disagree with your friends when they want to do something you feel is wrong? Why? Why not? _____

_____

_____

As a very young man, Jesus spoke in his hometown synagogue. He was not too well received, for many local people were envious of him. Yet this is what we read in the gospel (Luke 4:16–19, 28–29):

[Jesus] came to Nazareth, where he had been brought up, and went into the synagogue on the sabbath day as he usually did. He stood up to read, and they handed

him the scroll of the prophet Isaiah. Unrolling the
scroll he found the place where it is written:
> The Spirit of the Lord has been given to me,
> for he has anointed me.
> He has sent me to bring the good news to the
> poor,
> to proclaim liberty to the captives
> and to the blind new sight,
> to set the downtrodden free,
> to proclaim the Lord's year of favor...

When they heard this everyone in the synagogue was
enraged. They sprang to their feet and hustled him out
of town.

What effect did the Spirit of God have on Jesus? _____

_____

_____

Do you think Jesus was courageous in this story? Why? ____

_____

_____

Do you ever find yourself in situations when you should
speak out? When are they? Do you speak? _____

_____

_____

_____

_____

_____

_____

_____

A Saint for Now

Dorothy Day
(1897–1980)

Dorothy Day was a real American. She was born just before this century began and lived through all the excitement and confusion of the next eighty years, through some of the most eventful periods in our history. In every twist and turn of our national journey, Dorothy was present speaking out for the gospel of Jesus. Even when others did not want to hear her, even when she was put in jail for her courageous words, Dorothy continued speaking.

Dorothy grew up unnoticed, graduated from college, became a respected journalist in New York City, and had a baby. Thus far, her life was not very different from other young women her age. She deeply loved the father of her child, but he did not believe in marriage and refused to have any ceremony of marriage at all.

Shortly after Tamar was born, Dorothy began to read about Jesus and about the Catholic church. Deep inside her, she knew that God was calling her to believe in Jesus and to become a member of the church which at the time numbered among its members many poor immigrants. When she discussed these desires with Tamar's father, he flew into a rage. He did not believe in God or in Jesus, and he despised the Catholic church.

No matter how much she begged or explained, he would not change. He refused to allow her to baptize Tamar or to become a Catholic. Faced with his opposition, Dorothy acted with courage. She took Tamar to be baptized, was baptized herself, and began a most unusual life in the Catholic church.

These were the days of the Great American Depression. Every street corner had people begging or selling a little fruit to stave off starvation. Never had so many Americans been so poor. Never had so many been so hungry.

Dorothy remembered that Jesus had said his followers should feed the hungry. With a few friends, she started the first soup kitchen where they fed hundreds of people. This was not enough for Dorothy. She remembered that Jesus had also said we should use our talents to help others, and so she started the newspaper *The Catholic Worker* to tell all America about the problems of the poor and what could be done to help them.

Not everyone was pleased with what Dorothy wrote. She took the gospel quite seriously and applied it with great courage to the everyday problems of her day. When the United States was preparing to enter World War II, she spoke out against all war. She said that all war was un-Christian and forbidden by the gospel. Many young men who followed her were put in jail when they refused to be drafted.

Through the war and after, Dorothy kept up her service to the poor, always feeding them, always demanding that society help them in their pain. She traveled across the United States starting Catholic Worker houses and soup kitchens. She spoke out against the abuse of the poor Mexican workers who planted and harvested crops in the U.S. She stood solidly against the Viet Nam War and begged presidents and cardinals to look at the gospel and reform their lives.

Dorothy died in 1980. People from all over the United States and the world attended her funeral. Many thought she had been a saint, a saint of courage in a difficult and confusing time. She had never hesitated to call her beloved country and her beloved church to a new way of life, a way of life more in keeping with the gospel of Jesus. She spent long hours each day in prayer and always had time to serve the most neglected of the world's poor.

Ideas to Discuss with Others

We can learn many important lessons from those who share our lives. To learn the lessons we must listen to their experiences and their wisdom. Parents, especially, are good sources for our growth in understanding. Here are a few questions you might like to ask others. When you hear their answers, ponder them during your quiet moments.

Questions for Your Parents
When you were my age did you ever feel embarrassed? What made you afraid? Were you ever afraid to speak out and say what you thought was right? How did you get the courage to say what you believed? Did confirmation help you do this?

Questions for a Teacher
Are you ever afraid? What things make you afraid? How will confirmation give us the courage to speak out? Do you think confirmation helps you in your work today?

Questions for a Friend
Do you ever feel embarrassed? When? Are you ever afraid? When? What do you do when you are embarrassed? Afraid?

Questions for God

What things do you want me to say to others? Where can I find the courage to speak out when I am afraid?

A Final Word

All of us admire courageous people who are not afraid to speak out. We sometimes like to dream of ourselves as great heroes who face any hardship rather than be silenced. We may imagine ourselves another Patrick Henry crying for liberty or death. Or we may dream of being like Dorothy Day, speaking out for the gospel even when this means going to jail and being laughed at by other people.

In everyday life we have many opportunities to speak out. In class we should ask the questions on our minds even though some might think us foolish for our openness. Very often our questions are also in the minds of others. When we ask the question, all benefit from the answer.

When our friends are talking about life and its problems, we have an opportunity to tell them about Jesus and how he brings joy into our day-to-day living. When our friends are wrong we can correct them. When they are right we can encourage them. While they might not always approve our forthrightness and might even be embarrassed by our words, they will come to admire and love us for the help we bring them.

We also need to have the courage to tell our parents how we feel about them. So often the only time we speak out to our parents is when we are angry. In our more peaceful moments, how often do we say "thank you" to them for all they do for us? How often do we compliment them on the sacrifices they make for the whole family?

Speaking out is a virtue, one that the Holy Spirit will help us develop. As you prepare for confirmation, practice being forthright and honest in your conversations with others. There is no better way to ask the Spirit to give you the courage to speak out for justice and truth.

5

Courage to Be Young

Have you ever read in the gospels that Jesus said we are to become like little children? If you have read this command of Jesus, you probably wondered why in the world Jesus would say something like that. After all, we spend most of our time trying not to act like little children. Our parents warn us not to act like babies. Our teachers tell us our behavior is too childish. Even our friends sometimes say we are acting immaturely. If there is one thing we are trying not to be, it is like little children.

Yet, Jesus must have something in mind when he says that we must become like little children. Jesus has all the wisdom of God and, more than anyone else, knows what he is talking about. If acting like a little child is good for him, there must be some good in it for us, too.

Perhaps the answer to our problem is understanding two words which look alike but mean something very different. The words are *childish* and *childlike*. Jesus wants us to be childlike and to put aside all our childishness. Let's see what all that means.

People are childish when they insist on having things their own way all the time. If you have younger brothers or sisters, you have seen them bawling their heads off because they could not play outside on a rainy day. Perhaps you can remember throwing a temper tantrum because you were not allowed to have a piece of candy. Children are always making a big thing over getting their own way. This kind of behavior is childish.

Now, some teenagers and even some adults behave in childish ways at times. A boy who loses his temper in a game is behaving childishly. A girl who blows up with her friends because they won't do what she wants is childish. An adult who becomes angry because his car won't start or because his golf shot goes awry is behaving childishly.

This kind of behavior is very self-centered, even selfish. It is very unlike what we mean when we say that someone is childlike. The childlike person imitates the best quality of the young. Little children never worry very long. They have such trust in their parents that they can put aside any concern and relax. They know that their parents will care for them and protect them from evil.

Being childlike is having this kind of confidence in God. When Jesus asks us to be childlike, he is saying that we should have complete trust in God. We are not to worry about our hair, our complexion, our friendships with others, or our lack of success in school. Rather, we are to place all these possible anxieties in the hands of God and allow to direct and guide our lives.

Trusting God is not as simple as it sounds. Learning to trust takes many years. We have to work at developing this virtue day-by-day. We can begin by turning over our small worries to God—and then our larger ones. To do this, we will need help. In confirmation the Holy Spirit will give us that help, breathing into our hearts the courage to be always young, always childlike, with God, our parent and our friend.

Thinking About Our Worries

1. Do you worry about any of the following?

	Yes	No	Why
Catching AIDS	___	___	___
The size of your feet	___	___	___
Blemishes on your skin	___	___	___
The condition of your hair	___	___	___
Whether friends like you	___	___	___
Success in athletics	___	___	___
Success in school	___	___	___
Going to heaven/hell	___	___	___
Your parents' death	___	___	___
Your future	___	___	___
Your popularity	___	___	___
The condition of the world	___	___	___

2. Can you think of other things you sometimes worry about? List them, and next to each write why you worry about them.

My Worries	Why I Worry
_____	_____
_____	_____
_____	_____

3. What do you do when you become worried?_____
_____
_____

4. Write a prayer asking God to help you overcome your worries and to grow in trust of God's loving care for you.

_____

_____

_____

_____

_____

_____

_____

5. Put a check next to the things worry does to harm you:

___ Makes me nervous

___ Makes me depressed

___ Makes me sad and irritable

___ Puts a strain on my friendships

___ Distracts me from my work

___ Ruins my disposition

6. Can you think of anything good that worry does for you?

_____

_____

Prayers

A Prayer for Happiness

God, our parent and friend,
We come today to ask for your help.
We want to be true followers of
    your son, Jesus.
We believe what he has taught us.
We believe you want us to be happy.

But it is not easy to be a Christian.
People laugh and make fun of our ideals,
    just as they laughed at Jesus.
Help us resist the temptation
    to settle for less than
    the true happiness you have promised us.
Through your son, Jesus,
Our Lord and our brother.
Amen.

A Prayer for Sensitivity

God, our good and gentle parent,
Our world is filled with signs of your goodness.
    The stars shine on us each night.
    The sun warms our bodies and our minds.
    The earth gives us food and a place to live.
Open our eyes to see what is all around us.
Give us the sensitivity to your work which will lead us
    to thank you and to praise your great glory.
We ask you this through Jesus, our Lord and our
    brother.
Amen.

Bible Readings

Here are two short readings from the Bible to help you
think more about the courage to be young that the Holy
Spirit will bring to you in confirmation.

One day Jesus' disciples asked him who would be the
greatest in the Kingdom of God. They expected that he
would tell them they were to be the greatest. Instead, he did

something very unexpected. St. Matthew reports it this way (18:1–4):

> At this time the disciples came to Jesus and said, "Who is the greatest in the kingdom of heaven?" So he called a little child to him and set the child in front of them. Then he said, "I tell you solemnly, unless you change and become like little children you will never enter the kingdom of heaven. And so, the one who makes himself as little as this child is the greatest in the kingdom of heaven."

How do you think the disciples felt when they heard Jesus' answer to their question? ————————————————

————————————————————————————————

Do you think you are becoming more and more like a little child in your relationship with God? Why? Why not?

————————————————————————————————

————————————————————————————————

How will the Holy Spirit help you become more like a little child in confirmation? ————————————————

————————————————————————————————

————————————————————————————————

Jesus taught this idea of becoming like a little child in another way when he said (Matthew 6:25–29):

> That is why I am telling you not to worry about your life and what you are to eat, nor about your body and

how you are to clothe it. Surely life means more than food, and the body more than clothing! Look at the birds in the sky. They do not sow or reap or gather into barns; yet your heavenly Father feeds them. Are you not worth much more than they are? Can any of you, for all your worrying, add one single cubit to your span of life? And why worry about clothing? Think of the flowers growing in the fields; they never have to work or spin; yet I assure you that not even Solomon in all his regalia was robed like one of these.

In your own words, jot down what Jesus teaches in this passage from the gospels. _____

_____

_____

Will God care for us in everything? Why? Why not?_____

_____

_____

Do you ever think of this teaching when you are worried?

_____

_____

_____

A Saint for Now

John Vianney, Curé d'Ars
(1786–1859)

Everyone said that John was a dull peasant boy. No one expected he would ever amount to anything. When John was a child, attending Mass was against the law in France. Priests had to move from town to town and celebrate Mass secretly in someone's home or barn. There the people who really believed in Jesus would gather to pray together. If they were caught by the police, they would be fined or even put into prison.

John and his family went to Mass every chance they had and never seemed to worry very much about being put into jail or having to pay a large fine. Like his parents, John knew what was right to do and did it. He left the rest to God. This was the way his life began and the way it developed year after year.

When John was a young man he was drafted into the army. John was not an apt soldier. He was clumsy and awkward and never seemed to be able to get into the spirit of war. Other soldiers laughed at this unlikely recruit and despaired of ever making a soldier of him. John prayed, smiled, and went his way. He did not seem to worry about it at all.

One day while on maneuvers, John was separated from his company. He was lost and confused. Some friendly villagers took him in and hid him from the police who were seeking him because he had left the army. In the midst of all this danger, John was calm and peaceful. He had placed himself in God's care and seemed able to let God direct his life.

When the war was over, John came out of hiding and tried to put his life back together. He thought he would like to become a priest since the laws had been changed and Mass attendance was now permitted. Everyone warned John that it was not possible for him to become a priest since he had little schooling and was not smart enough to make up for the lost time. John listened to all this advice and decided to try in spite of it.

For years he was made fun of by younger students, humiliated by teachers, and almost dismissed from more than one seminary. Yet, there was something very good about young John that impressed those who directed the seminaries he attended. They noticed that he was like a little child in his confidence in God. He never seemed upset or worried. Instead, he prayed and did the best he could.

After many trials, John was ordained a priest. The bishop sent him to a very poor country parish, an assignment other priests wanted to avoid. The people in the village of Ars had a reputation for being very hardhearted and irreligious. They had not had a priest for a long time and really did not want one. John was not afraid, however. He placed his trust in God and went to the village of Ars.

There a wonderful thing happened. John's goodness slowly influenced the poor village people. One by one they came to understand the simplicity and greatness of this childlike priest. Before long, Ars had a reputation for being one of the holiest villages in all of France. From all over Europe, men and women came to pray in the little parish church and to talk with the pastor, whom everyone said was already a saint.

John Vianney was never blessed with beauty or high intelligence. What he did have was a complete trust in God. Because he could trust God this completely, he was able to overcome all obstacles to his goals and, in the process, to become one of France's greatest saints.

Ideas to Discuss with Others

We can learn many important lessons from those who share

our lives. To learn, we must listen to their experiences and their wisdom. Parents, especially, are good sources for our growth in trust. Here are a few questions you might like to ask others. When you hear their answers, ponder them during your quiet moments.

Questions for Your Parents

Do you often worry about life? What do you do when you are filled with worries? Do you pray to God about your worries? Does this help you overcome them or not? Do you ever worry about me? What do you do when you are worried about me?

Questions for a Teacher

What does it mean to trust another person? How do you learn to trust people? Is it hard? Is there anything we can do to learn how to trust? In confirmation, will the Holy Spirit help us learn to trust?

Questions for a Friend

What people in your life do you trust the most? Do you ever regret you trusted anyone? Do you think you trust God?

Questions for God

How can I learn to trust you more completely? How can I learn to become like a little child?

A Final Word

Confirmation brings us a deepened relationship with the Holy Spirit. Every good relationship in our lives helps us change and grow. Our relationship with the Holy Spirit is no exception. After confirmation, we should have the power to become more fully grown and more closely united to God.

One of the ways we can measure that growth is our ability to trust God. All of our lives are filled with little problems and some lives are marked with great problems. Whether our problems are great or small, we must learn to trust that God will help us find a way to cope with them.

Jesus told us not to worry about such fundamental things as food and clothing. How much more important is it not to worry about little things like the size of our feet, the beauty of our complexion, and the condition of our hair. If God promises to help us find food and clothing, how much more will we be able to cope with little problems like these?

Worrying about life does nothing to make it better. In fact, worry makes us sad and anxious. Worry brings us to depression and depression leads us to forget what a wonderful gift life itself really is. The person who becomes like a little child and learns to trust in God will slowly put aside worries and lead a happy, carefree life. Holiness is happiness. Yes, Jesus' message is as simple as that.

6

Courage to Be Friends

Something wonderful happens to us in adolescence. That something wonderful is friends. As children, our entire focus in life is our family. Even our playmates fit or don't fit into our lives because of our families. This is all as it should be, for as little children our need for our family is so great nothing can be allowed to interfere with it.

As we grow up, however, our lives begin to focus away from our families. This does not happen all at once. There are many times when family must come first. Yet, there are other times when family relationships are not quite enough. We need to supplement our family love with love from those we call our friends.

Beginning in junior high and continuing well into the young adult years, our greatest task in life is to find friends and build good relationships with them. At first our friends are usually members of our own sex. Later we begin to make friendships with members of the opposite sex. Finally, one of those relationships may mature into marriage, which could become the foundation of our adult life. Making friends, then, is the root of our future happiness.

Many teens experience great difficulty in learning to relate to other people. We say they are shy or that they don't seem interested in others or that they are unsure and hesitant with people. Not everyone can be outgoing and immediately friendly. Our personalities are all different.

Some of the problems we experience are rooted in the fickleness of our friends. One day, we think a particular person is our very best friend. Then, almost without our realizing it, our friendship breaks apart. We discover ourselves alone. When this happens, we wish our friends were more loyal and true to us. Do we ever question ourselves, however, on how loyal and true we are to our friends?

Another problem in making friends is finding people who are open to new friends. So often teens live in comfortable little cliques. These small groups say to everyone around, "No Admittance." When we are on the outside, we resent such behavior. We think it unfair of others to live in such a closed way. Yet, is it possible that we sometimes give that impression to others? Do we sometimes say that we are not interested in others joining our special groups?

A final reason friendships are hard to make is that all people are different from one another. When a person is less popular, less handsome, less skillful or poorer than others, it is very difficult for that person to find friends. People like to be friends with those who have many talents, but often ignore the less talented.

In confirmation we say that the Holy Spirit deepens in us the virtue of charity or love. This charity is the glue which bonds us to other people as well as to God. Confirmation, then, can help us in forming our friendships. It can help us develop greater loyalty, more openness, and can open our eyes to the needs of those who are not like us.

Friendship is a very holy thing. It reflects, in its way, the inner life of God. Just as the three persons are united together and form one God, so friends, in their way, mirror this unity among persons. Because friendship is so important, God assists us in forming good friendships if we will allow God to do so. In the weeks before confirmation, pray for your friends and pray, too, for all the people not yet your friends who need you.

Thinking About Friends

1. Who are your four best friends?

   a. _____

   b. _____

   c. _____

   d. _____

2. What do you admire most about them?

   a. _____

   b. _____

   c. _____

   d. _____

3. What do you think your friends admire about you?

_____

_____

4. How loyal are your friends? _____

5. Are you and your friends open to other people joining your group? Why do you say this? _____

_____

6. Do you ever feel unpopular and alone? _____
When? _____

_____

7. How can you make friends with those who have no close
friends? _____

_____

_____

8. In the space below write a prayer to the Holy Spirit about
your friends. _____

_____

_____

_____

_____

_____

_____

Prayers

Does Anyone Need Me, God?

Does anyone really need me, God?
Does someone really want me to lend a hand?
Will this someone understand
That it's all so new to me?
Will I say the right things, do the right things?
Where do I begin?
Please help me, God.
Help me to begin to be a friend.
Amen.

For My Friends

My friends are very special people, God.
I know you will agree.
My friends are very special people, God.
They mean everything to me.
My friends are very special people, God.
They search my heart with me.
My friends are very special people, God.
They help me look beyond myself and see.
My friends are very special people, God.
Bless them all you can.
My friends are very special people, God.
Help us live life as you plan.
Amen.

Bible Readings

Here are two short readings from the Bible to help you think more about your friendships.

In his letter to the Galatians (5:13–16, 22), Saint Paul told what happens to those who receive the Holy Spirit. After reading the passage, think of what these words mean to you and your friends.

Serve one another…in works of love, since the whole of the Law is summarized in a single command: Love your neighbor as yourself. If you go snapping at each other and tearing each other to pieces, you had better watch or you will destroy the whole community.
    Let me put it like this: if you are guided by the Spirit

you will be in no danger of yielding to self-indulgence....What the Spirit brings is very different: love, joy, peace, patience, kindness, goodness, trustfulness, gentleness, and self-control.

Do people you know sometimes snap at one another? _____
If so, why do you think they do this?_____
_____
_____

What does this do to friendships? _____
_____
_____

How many of the gifts of the spirit listed in the reading above do you see in yourself? _____
_____
_____

How do these things help you make friends?_____
_____
_____

In another of his letters (First Letter to the Corinthians 13: 4–7), Saint Paul tells us what happens to us when we learn to love our friends.

Love is always patient and kind; it is never jealous; love is never boastful or conceited; it is never rude or selfish; it does not take offense, and is not resentful.

Love takes no pleasure in other people's sins but delights in the truth; it is always ready to excuse, to trust, to hope and to endure whatever comes.

When are you patient and kind to your friends? _____

_____

_____

Are you ever jealous? When? _____

_____

_____

Are your friends patient and kind to you? When? When not? _____

_____

_____

Are they ever jealous? When? _____

_____

_____

In how many other ways are your friendships like what Saint Paul describes in this reading? _____

_____

_____

Are there some ways your friendships are not like this reading? How? _____

_____

_____

_____

A Saint for Now

Ignatius of Loyola
(1491–1556)

Ignatius was born to be a soldier, and a soldier he became. He loved the excitement of battle and the joy of comradeship in the army. While he was still a young man, Ignatius's career came to an abrupt end. He was struck by a cannonball and left lame. During the months of confinement while his wounds were mending, Ignatius read about the saints because there were no other books available to read. The more he read, the more he desired to become a saint.

Once he was able to walk again, Ignatius went back to school. He had had little formal education and so had to start with the beginners. The beginners were very young compared to this lame older man. Year after year Ignatius studied in school after school. Everywhere he made friends with men years younger than he. Perhaps his respect for others won Ignatius so many friends.

As Ignatius was nearing the end of his studies, he went to the University of Paris, at the time the greatest school in all of Europe. There Ignatius met many new friends. One young man Ignatius tried to befriend resisted him stoutly. That man was Francis Xavier.

The reason Francis did not want to be friends with Ignatius was Ignatius's holiness. If there was one thing Francis did not want to be, it was some religious fanatic. He wanted to finish his studies and become a teacher. Perhaps one day he might even write a great book and even become the president of the University. Francis was ambitious, and friendship with Ignatius would not help further his ambitions.

Still Ignatius was patient. One day he asked Francis Xavier what he planned to do.

"I'll finish my degree and begin to teach," Francis replied stiffly.

"Ah," said Ignatius, "what then?"

"Why, I'll write books and become president of the University."

"Ah," said Ignatius with a smile, "what then?"

"By then, I shall be old and rich and will enjoy myself a bit."

"Ah, what then?"

"Then I shall die I suppose, you foolish old man."

"Ah," said Ignatius with a twinkle in his eye, "what then?"

"You had better stop your foolish questions and leave me alone," Francis blurted out. "All you do is trouble me and upset my life." With that, he stalked away in anger.

Meanwhile, Ignatius prayed for young Francis. He wanted him to become one of his companions. He wanted him to join with his other friends in a great effort to save the church during one of its most troubled ages.

Later Ignatius and his friends were about to make a solemn pledge to serve Jesus and to remain loyal to one another. Still Francis was not with them. Each time Ignatius saw Francis he smiled and began, "Ah, what...." Francis always stalked away angrily.

Just as Ignatius and his other friends were about to leave Paris and go to Rome to begin their work, Francis gave in. He rushed to Ignatius and the others and joined them. Happily all set out for Rome together. They called themselves the Company of Jesus. Today, we know the order they started as the Jesuits.

Of all the members of the happy group, Francis and Ignatius were the closest friends. Years later, Ignatius sent Francis to the Far East to preach the message of Jesus. Even at so great a distance, the two friends kept in touch by frequent letters.

It is this same kind of friendship with our peers the Spirit of God can help us achieve when he comes to us in confirmation.

Ideas to Discuss with Others

We can learn many important lessons from those who share our lives. To learn the lessons we must listen to their experiences and their wisdom. Parents, especially, are good sources for our growth. Here are a few questions you might like to ask others. When you hear their answers, ponder them during your quiet moments.

Questions for Your Parents
Did you have friends when you were my age? Who were they? What were they like? Who was your best friend? What sort of things did you do together? Did you ever get into arguments? How did you solve your problems?

Questions for a Teacher
What does it mean to be a friend? What things do you most admire in your friends? Do your friends ever disappoint you? What do you do when this happens? Do you ever have to give up on a friend?

Questions for a Friend
Why do you think we are friends? Do you think we ever ex-

clude others from our friendship? What can we do to help other people our own age?

Questions for God

Do you really want me to be your friend? How can I show you how much I value your friendship?

A Final Word

Our friendships are very important to us. Because they are important to us, they are also important to God. God cares about the friends we make and how we grow because of our friends, wants us to learn to love others so that we will know better how to love God. For this and many other reasons, God gives us the help we need to mature in our relationships with others.

In confirmation, the Spirit reaffirms God's life within us. Once we understand who is within us, we are free to make other friends. Our other friends can help us grow closer to God. In fact, friendship is one of the best ways to grow closer to God provided, of course, our friends are good people.

Jesus once said that when we look out for our own life we will lose it, but when we give up our life for his sake we can be sure to find it. At first these sound like very strange words. They seem to contradict each other. But when we think about them a little while we can see that they contain great wisdom. What Jesus said about our friendship with him is true of our friendship with others.

The more we try to get our own way and to use our friends to please ourselves, the more sure we can be of losing them. Only when we stop thinking about ourselves and let other people have their way some of the time can we find friendship. Our happiness in life depends on our ability to make and keep friends. Our holiness depends on much the same thing. After all, it is when we make sacrifices for our friends that we become holy. Jesus tells us that one day we will be strong enough to make sacrifices even for our enemies. When this happens, our understanding of friendship will be complete.

7

Belonging to the Church

No one likes to be alone, even alone with God, all of the time. We like other people. We need other people, people to talk with us, to listen to our dreams, to ask us questions, to share with us and, at times, to simply be with us quietly. We are most comfortable with people who share our highest ideals. This sharing makes it easy for us to talk and builds a sense of being comfortable we call *community*.

A good example of people with whom we are comfortable is our family. Now, we may argue and disagree about many things but when all is said and done we are united together by love, by experiences we have shared together, and by some common ideals and beliefs about life. The more love, the more common experiences, and the more we share ideals, the closer is our family life.

Similarly, the more comfortable we are with our friends, the more community we share with them. We love our friends. We have shared many experiences with them— experiences like going to school, attending ball games, talking together, and maybe even more. We also share ideals even when we do not express them, for we pick our friends from people who look at life much as we do.

The church is another example of a group of people who are comfortable with one another, people who are a community. We are comfortable with our fellow church members because we love them and care what happens to them. If someone is sick, we pray for her. If someone is in need, we share our resources with this person. If someone is troubled, we counsel him. All day long, our parish is responding to the needs of its people because all of us care about one another.

Then, too, we all have some similar experiences. We all believe in Jesus. We all go to Mass together on Sunday. Those who are older share a similar religious education. Many of our experiences are so much alike.

Finally, all of us share ideals. We believe the world should be a fair and decent place in which to live. We know that all people are our brothers and sisters. Everyone should have enough to eat, a place to live, a chance to gain an education, an opportunity to worship God and live happily in one great human family.

Our parents and other adults often tell us that the Catholic church is a good place to discover how we can love God and the whole human family. Some young people wonder whether loving God and the whole human family is really important for them and their happiness. Other things seem more important, things like being popular, getting good grades in school, and having a good time. With all the pressures young people feel, it is often difficult to find time to think about God and the human family.

Growing into a love for God, the church, and the human family takes time. Confirmation is a kind of promise by the adult community of faith that it will care for its younger members and wait for them to awaken to a deeper love.

Your parish community promises to love you and to stand by you during your years of change and growth. It also promises to try to share its faith with you and to listen to you as you fashion a faith all your own.

Confirmation will help you learn how to relate happily to that community of faith. The Spirit promises to warm your heart with a deeper love for God, for the human family, and for the community of faith we call the church. You will sense that the community of faith is a wonderful place to be, that the human family needs your care and concern, and that God is always at your side.

These new and deeper thoughts may come to you in an instant as they did with Saint Paul. More likely, they will dawn on you only slowly as you wend your way toward adult faith. Meanwhile, your task is to pray for that awakening and to love God, the human family, and the community of faith the best you can.

Thinking About the Church

1. In the spaces below list the things you find helpful to you in the church:

a. _____ b. _____
c. _____ d. _____
e. _____ f. _____

2. In the spaces below list the things about church which you find difficult:

a. _____ b. _____
c. _____ d. _____
e. _____ f. _____

3. What things do you have in common with others in your parish?

a. _____   b. _____

c. _____   d. _____

e. _____   f. _____

4. What experiences have you shared with them?

a. _____   b. _____

c. _____   d. _____

e. _____   f. _____

5. What could you do to get more out of belonging to the church?

a. _____   b. _____

c. _____   d. _____

e. _____   f. _____

6. In the space below sketch a picture of your parish church.

7. After looking at your picture, write a prayer for all the
people who worship there. _____

_____

_____

_____

_____

_____

Prayers

To the Holy Spirit

God, our kind and loving friend,
We thank you for sending your Holy Spirit
   to guide our foreparents in the early church.
We thank you, too, for the Spirit's presence among us,
   as we struggle to understand what it is to be
   a Christian today,
   a person worthy of such a heritage.
Amen.

The Church

O Jesus,
I want to be a member of your church.
I want to share in that great community of men and women
   of all ages who care about you and
   about their neighbors.
I want to be faithful to the teaching of the apostles,
   to the community,
   to the breaking of the bread and
   to the prayers.

Sometimes, however, this is not easy.
I see about me men and women who wear your name
 and still
 are filled with hardness, callousness, and contempt.
I do not want to be one with them.
Help me look beyond the pettiness of people
 to the true unity of believers
 where you are always present,
 for they are gathered in your name. Amen.

Bible Readings

Here are two short readings from the Bible to help you think about your membership in the church.

The first generation of believers lived in community. Their daily life is described in this passage from the Acts of the Apostles (2:42, 44–47):

These [the early Christians] remained faithful to the teaching of the apostles, to the brotherhood, to the breaking of the bread and to the prayers....

The faithful all lived together and owned everything in common; they sold their goods and possessions and shared out the proceeds among themselves according to what each one needed.

They went as a body to the Temple every day but met in their houses for the breaking of bread; they shared their food gladly and generously; they praised God and were looked up to by everyone.

1. Would you like to have been a member of this group? Why? _____

_____

_____

_____

2. In what ways is your parish like the early church?

_____

_____

_____

3. Are there things you can do to make your parish more like the early church? What are they? _____

_____

_____

_____

Saint Paul loved the church. He loved it so much that he saw it as the body of Christ, men and women united so closely they seemed to be a single body with Jesus as its head. This is what he said (First Letter to the Corinthians 12:12, 13, 27):

Just as a human body, though it is made up of many parts, is a single unit because all these parts, though many, make one body, so it is with Christ. In the one Spirit we were all baptized, Jews as well as Greeks, slaves as well as citizens, and one Spirit was given to us all to drink....

Now you together are Christ's body; but each of you is a different part of it.

1. Can you see why Paul said we were the body of Christ?

_____

2. In what ways do we work together as the parts of a body work together? _____

_____

3. All parts of the human body are enlivened by one soul. What enlivens all parts of the body of Christ?_____

_____

_____

4. All parts of the body care for one another. How do we show our care for other members of the church? _____

_____

_____

A Saint for Now

Catherine of Siena
(1347–1380)

Catherine was a most unusual young woman. The twenty-third child in her family, she was unlike any of her brothers and sisters. From the time she was very young, Catherine wanted to find a special way to live. Her mother wanted her to marry or become a nun. Catherine wanted neither of these lifestyles. Instead, she determined to remain single and to devote her full energy to serving the church. In the fourteenth century when Catherine lived, this style of life was not approved.

Gradually Catherine convinced her parents that God was calling her to this unusual vocation. Her father set aside one room in their house for Catherine's special use. In a family of 23 children, this was not easy to do, but Catherine's father believed in her and her special calling.

For several years Catherine fasted and prayed. People wondered what was to become of this young girl with the very different style of life. Each morning she arose early and began her day with hours of prayer. Later, she attended Mass at the local church. Then she returned to prayer where she spent the rest of her waking hours. Catherine was so very different from the other young girls who lived in Siena.

Gradually other people, young and old, men and women, began to notice Catherine and asked to talk with her. Catherine was a forthright person, one who never minced words. Many liked her straight talk and found her a trustworthy guide to God. Quickly those who had experienced Catherine's friendship began to band together to form a kind of family of their own. Soon priests and laypeople, men and women, young and old, were a part of Catherine's special family. They spent long hours in prayer together, enjoyed being together at meals, and looked for ways to serve other people.

Catherine and her "family" were very concerned about injustice and war. They became deeply involved in politics for they wanted to bring peace and justice to their town. Others laughed at them at first but later had to take them seriously because they had such a wide following among the people of Siena. From prayer, then, Catherine and her friends turned to politics and were as successful at the one as at the other.

The high point of Catherine's life came when she visited

Pope Gregory XI. He was living not in Rome where he should have been but in a French village, because he was afraid of his enemies. Catherine spoke boldly to Pope Gregory. She insisted that he have the courage to face his enemies and return to Rome. He hesitated, so great was his fear of conflict. When the pope looked at this fearless woman and listened to her challenge him, he knew that God was speaking to him through Catherine. After a long inner battle, Gregory heeded Catherine's advice and returned to Rome.

All through her life Catherine had many friends. These men and women shared her ideals and her experience of faith. They all cared for one another and for Catherine. In a sense, they were the church living in Siena. From their friendship came a strong cry for justice and peace in the world. From their support of Catherine came a strong voice to reform the larger church.

Today, centuries after her death, the people of Siena revere Catherine as one of the greatest people in their history. They look back and wish they had been a part of her special family. We, too, would like to be a part of such a group, and we can be. The church in every age is the family of God, the community of those who believe in Jesus and care for one another.

Ideas to Discuss with Others

We can learn many important lessons from those who share our lives. To learn these lessons we must listen to their experiences and their wisdom. Parents, especially, are good sources for our understanding of the church. Here are a few questions you might like to ask others. When you hear their answers, ponder them during your quiet moments.

Questions for Your Parents

Do you enjoy going to Mass on Sunday? What kind of feelings do you have during the Mass? Do you feel at home in our parish? Do you think people in our parish like us? Do we or did we ever belong to a parish where everyone seemed warm and friendly?

Questions for a Teacher

Why do you give up your time to help prepare for confirmation? Do you enjoy going to Mass on Sunday? Do you think God will reward you for what you are doing for us? Are there other reasons you are a teacher?

Questions for a Friend

Do you think we are members of a clique? Do we exclude others from our friendship? What are your feelings about our parish?

Questions for God

Why have you called me to be a Catholic? What can I do to feel more at home in my church?

A Final Word

Like all the sacraments, confirmation comes to us in the church. The community of those who believe in Jesus is always the setting for a sacrament. God wants us to love God through our fellow believers.

One of the special gifts the Spirit of God brings to us is charity or love. That love reaches out to all people but especially to the people who pray with us each week. Our concern for the elderly begins with those who are a part of our spiritual family. Our concern for the poor starts in the family of God.

This does not mean that what starts here ends here. On the contrary, when we have learned to love those who are most like us, we are then prepared to love those who do not share as much with us. Like those in Catherine's "family," we reach out into politics and into the wider world to help bring justice and peace.

Confirmation is about our loving others. To be ready for this sacrament, we should spend some time helping other people. If your parish has a program for helping others, by all means join it. If it does not, begin by doing things to help your own parents, your brothers and sisters, the people who are in school with you. The world is filled with men and women, boys and girls, who need what only you can bring. This loving of others is the root of all Christian life and especially at the heart of the sacrament of confirmation.

8

Say It in Prayer

Friends like to be together. It has always been that way. In the Old Testament we can read about the time the friends Jonathan and David spent with each other. In the New Testament we can read about the weeks and months Jesus and the apostles spent talking, listening, and just being together.

What was true in Bible days is still true today. Think how much time you spend with your friends. Much of the time is spent doing nothing special. You may sit on a set of stairs and hardly talk at all. You may go to a basketball game together and hardly say a word during the game. You may go to a movie together and spend hours without talking at all. Yet the time spent on the stairs or at the basketball game or the movie is somehow better time, richer time, because you have friends with you.

Whether we are talking about people in the Bible or people today, friends need time to be together. The same thing is true in our friendship with God. We need to spend time with God, not necessarily time saying long prayers, but quiet time just listening and being together.

Saint John Vianney told the story of a man he noticed in the church one morning. That afternoon he saw the same man in the same place in the church. John Vianney asked him if he had been there all day. The man replied that he had. The saint said, "What have you been doing all day here in the church?"

"Oh," the man replied, "I just look at God and God looks at me."

That is the highest form of prayer, just looking at God and letting God look at us. Of course, we cannot get to that kind of prayer right away. We must practice other forms of prayer in order to build up to that kind of intimacy with God.

One way to begin our prayer is to read a short passage from the Gospels and then talk to God about it in our own words. We can ask questions and listen for answers. We can express our pleasure with all God has given us, express our wonder, and then become quiet to see what God has to say to us about our own lives.

Another way to listen to God is to examine our consciences each day before we go to sleep. With God, we can look back over our day to see what kind of life we led. When we notice times during the day when we were irritable, selfish, or unkind, we can tell God how sorry we are and then listen for some response.

A third way of learning to pray is to talk a little and then listen a little. At almost any quiet time during our day, we can talk to God about the things most important to us and then spend a few moments listening. By repeating this process often during our day, we can soon become people of deep prayer.

Now, God does not speak to us in exactly the same way our friends or parents do. Our listening must be very attentive and very still. Sometimes we will hear nothing at all. At other times we will be sure we know that God is communicating to us, not so much in words but in our hearts. Words are not so important. Our deepest feelings are important, however, and it is through them that God often speaks to us.

Confirmation is only the beginning of a new and more intense life with God. It will be such a beginning only if we learn to pray.

Thinking About God

1. How do you feel when you think about you and Jesus together? _____

_____

_____

_____

2. When do you feel very close to Jesus and his Holy Spirit?

_____

_____

_____

3. Where do you feel close to Jesus and his Holy Spirit?

_____

_____

_____

4. When you pray, what things do you talk about with God?

_____

_____

_____

5. What was the most important thing that happened to you today?_____

_____

_____

_____

6. Make up a prayer about this event._____

_____

_____

_____

_____

_____

_____

Prayers

Talking to God About Prayer

God, my kind and loving friend,
I have reflected today on my need for prayer
   and how I am to learn to pray.
I come to you, united with your Son, Jesus,
   to seek your help in establishing a daily time for prayer,
   in finding a quiet place for this daily prayer.
I seek your help, too, in directing me to simple things
   which will make my prayer sincere, humble, and full
   of faith.
I ask you this through Jesus, my Lord and my brother.
Amen.

The Bible

O God, who caused all the Holy Scriptures
   to be written for our learning:
Grant that we may in such wise hear them,
   read, mark, learn, and inwardly digest them,
that by patience and comfort of the holy Word,
   we may embrace and ever hold fast
the blessed hope of everlasting life,
   which you have given us in Jesus Christ.
Amen.

Book of Common Prayer

Bible Readings

Here are two short readings from the Bible to help you
think more about prayer:

One day the disciples of Jesus asked him to teach them
how to pray. This is how he answered them (Matthew
6:7–13):

In your prayers do not babble as the pagans do, for
they think that by using many words they will make
themselves heard. Do not be like them; your Father
knows what you need before you ask him. So you
should pray like this:
   Our Father in heaven,
   may your name be held holy,
   your kingdom come,
   your will be done,
   on earth as in heaven.
   Give us today our daily bread.
   And forgive us our debts,

as we have forgiven those who are in debt to us.
And do not put us to the test,
but save us from the evil one.

How do you feel when you say this prayer? _____
_____

Who is in debt to you? _____

Do you forgive these debts? Why? _____
_____
_____

What tests do you wish to be free from? _____
_____

Why? _____
_____

What do you need from God today? _____
_____
_____

Jesus told us that whatever we ask of God the Father in his
name will be given to us. These are his words (Luke 11:9–
13):

So I say to you: Ask, and it will be given to you; search,
and you will find; knock, and the door will be opened
to you. For the one who asks always receives; the one

who searches always finds; the one who knocks will always have the door opened to him. What father among you would hand his son a stone when he asked for bread? Or hand him a snake instead of a fish? Or hand him a scorpion if he asked for an egg? If you then, who are evil, know how to give your children what is good, how much more will the heavenly Father give the Holy Spirit to those who ask him!

In what ways do we search, ask, and knock when we pray?

_____

_____

Why do we believe God listens to us when we pray? _____

_____

_____

What did you pray for today?_____

_____

_____

Did God seem to answer your prayer? Why? Why not?_____

_____

_____

How do you feel about prayer today?_____

_____

_____

_____

A Saint for Now

Aloysius Gonzaga
(1568–1591)

Luigi was born to be a prince of the Holy Roman Empire. His family was one of the most violent and crafty in a violent and unholy age. Two of his brothers were murdered. All around him was the most terrifying brutality and open crime, for in those days the nobles of Italy were allowed to do exactly as they pleased. There was no government strong enough to insist that they respect the rights of other people.

When Luigi, as he called himself, was only seven years old, he discovered prayer. He liked to say the prayers he learned from his mother, even though he did not completely understand their meaning. While the adults of the court were involved in every kind of intrigue, young Luigi spent his days growing up to enjoy praying.

When Luigi was a young adolescent, he read two books which were important to him, one by a Jesuit priest, Gaspar Loarte, and one by Louis of Granada. In these two books, Luigi discovered how to pray silently, how to listen to God. With no one to guide him and few to show any interest in his inward journey, Luigi still practiced praying every day.

Soon Luigi began to read the lives of the saints. Here he found companions for his imagination and a sense that he was not alone. The lives of the saints inspired him to even greater efforts to learn to pray. Soon Luigi ignored court life entirely and spent long hours each day in prayer.

When he was 12 years old, Luigi received his first communion. (This was the age at which children received communion for the first time in those days.) Once he had received communion, Luigi developed a great interest in the eucharist. He loved to visit the chapel in his father's palace and spend long periods of time praying there.

Luigi's interest in prayer, reading, and the lives of the saints did not keep him from noticing the excitement of court life. All around him were intrigue, violence and brutality. Yet, in spite of all this, Luigi remained calm and determined to live his own kind of life.

While still very young, he announced to his father that he planned to give up his right to be a prince and instead to become a priest. His father was violently angry. Two of his sons had already been murdered and now this boy, his oldest son, was determined to leave home and reject everything which mattered most to him. Luigi's father refused him permission to enter the seminary. Luigi smiled but refused to change his intention. For seven years the two men, father and son, refused to give in to each other.

Finally Luigi had his way and entered the seminary in Rome. There all his fellow students loved the happy boy who had once been a prince. They admired his interest in his studies and his ability to pray quietly amid all kinds of excitement. He seemed to be always close to God and aware that God's spirit was within him.

Luigi's life was not only prayer and study. He also loved to help the poor. While he was still only 23 years old, Luigi spent day after day nursing the sick during an epidemic in Rome. In spite of his youth and strength, he caught the disease and died.

Luigi was soon thought of as a saint by his fellow students in Rome and by the poor people he had helped during his last days. When people began to write about him, his proud family insisted that he be called Aloysius instead of by his lifelong name Luigi. Today we know him as Saint Aloysius, the young boy and young man who learned to pray in circumstances which seem so adverse to any form of communion with God.

Ideas to Discuss with Others

We can learn many important lessons from those who share our lives. To learn these lessons we must listen to their experiences and their wisdom. Parents, especially, are good sources for our understanding of prayer. Here are a few questions you might like to ask others. When you hear their answers, ponder them during your quiet moments.

Questions for Parents
Did you pray very much when you were young? How did you pray? Did your parents ever talk to you about praying? What did they say to you? Is it easier or harder for you to pray now than it was when you were my age? Can we pray together some day? What prayers will we say?

Questions for a Teacher
What is your favorite prayer? Why do you like this prayer? What sort of prayers do you say each week? Do you find prayer helpful in your life? How do you help others learn to pray?

Questions for a Friend
Do you ever pray? Why do you like to pray? Who taught you about praying?

Questions for God
How can I learn to love you more and more? How can I speak to you without feeling self-conscious?

A Final Word

In a very short time, you will be confirmed in your faith. In a special way, the spirit of God will come to you and awaken you to a new depth of friendship with the three persons in God. Confirmation can be a beginning of a happier and holier life.

The key to becoming happier and holier is a spirit of prayer. Anyone can learn to pray. One does not have to be a great saint, highly intelligent, or a holier-than-thou sort of person. Prayer is as natural to our lives as breathing. It can occupy many small moments in our busy days. When it does, it is like a breath of fresh air clearing our minds and stimulating us to become friends not only with God but with all his people.

One writer said that prayer is like salt. Once you have established a habit of prayer, you will hardly notice that it is there. Only when you go without it will you realize how flat and tasteless life without God can become.

If there is one thing you can definitely bring to your own confirmation, it is a determination to pray daily. That determination will open for you a whole new life, a life filled with new friendships and new experiences of intimacy with God.

As you come to the end of this small journal, we who wrote it for you hope that you will indeed grow in prayer and that in your prayers you may sometimes remember all of us who have helped make your confirmation an event you may long remember.

Daily Prayers

Morning Prayers

The Sign of the Cross
Today I begin my waking moments in the name of the Father, and of the Son, and of the Holy Spirit.

A Morning Offering
Jesus,
I want to unite myself with Mary and the saints this
    morning and offer you my every thought, word and
    action.
May I bring glory to you and peace to all people.
May my life be one of gentleness and prayer.
May I shirk no duty.
May I love my family and my friends.
May this day be the best of days because it was spent
    with you.
Amen.

A Confirmation Prayer
Jesus, my friend,
    in a few short weeks I will be confirmed.
The Holy Spirit will come into my heart—
    the spirit of courage and prayer,
    the spirit of friendship and love,
    the spirit of wisdom and understanding.
Make my heart ready for this awesome coming.
Rid me of all selfishness and sin,
    of all fear and worry,
    of all pettiness and everything that is mean.

Ready me for my confirmation and a new and brighter
life ahead.
Amen.

A Prayer to Mary

Remember, most gracious Virgin Mary, that never was it
known that anyone who fled to your protection, implored
your help or sought your intercession was left unaided. Inspired with this confidence I fly unto you, O Virgin of vir-
gins, my Mother. To you do I come, before you I stand, sinful and sorrowful. O Mother of the Word Incarnate, despise
not my petitions, but in your mercy hear and answer me.
Amen.

The Holy Trinity Book of Prayers

The Lord's Prayer

Our Father, who art in heaven,
hallowed be thy name;
Thy kingdom come,
Thy will be done on earth as it is in heaven.
Give us this day our daily bread,
and forgive us our trespasses as
we forgive those who trespass against us;
lead us not into temptation,
but deliver us from evil.
Amen.

Evening Prayers

The Sign of the Cross

This evening I will begin my prayer in the name of the Father, and of the Son, and of the Holy Spirit.

Examination of My Day

Spend a few moments with Jesus looking back over your day. Where you are aware of thoughts, words, or actions that seem selfish or sinful, tell Jesus in your own words that you are sorry, and then say:

Jesus, my brother and my friend,
I am sorry for the times I thought only of myself,
for the times I never noticed the starving and suffering of our world.
For the times I wanted so much for myself that I forgot about my family.
For the times I used others to get my way and hardly noticed what I did to them.
For those words of mine which cut into the hearts of others and left them sad and trembling.
Help me, Jesus, to become more aware of others
and to worry less about myself.

The Hail Mary

Hail Mary, full of grace, the Lord is with you.
Blessed are you among women, and blessed is
the fruit of your womb, Jesus.
Holy Mary, Mother of God,
pray for us sinners, now and at the hour
of our death.
Amen.

Bill and Patty Coleman have written many books for people in the church. They have lived out their own confirmation pledge of concern for the poor and powerless in many ways. Both struggled for black rights in the civil rights movement. Later they worked in soup kitchens and in the peace movement. They now live and work among the poor in Cuernavaca, Mexico. They have three adult children and three grandchildren.